HO'OPONOPONO

Secrets

By Paul Jackson

Dedication

For Sarah my inspiration..
and Lilian my rock..

Table of Contents

Dedication iii

Introduction 1

Chapter 1: What is Ho'oponopono? Ho'oponopono & Universal Law........ 3

Chapter 2: Ho'oponopono Philosophy....................................... 15

Chapter 3: How It Works. Who Are We Really? Activating the Process.... 31

Chapter 4: Getting Started. The Four Phrases.................................... 39

Chapter 5: Ho'oponopono Practice & The Questions That Arise.............. 47

Chapter 6: Ho'oponopono and the Wider World 57

Chapter 7: Success with Ho'oponopono................................ 63

Chapter 8: Who's Who In Ho'oponopono? 67

Chapter 9: Other Ho'oponopono Tools....................................... 75

Chapter 10: Final Thoughts.. 77

Chapter 11: Inspiration, Thanks, & Acknowledgements 81

About the Author.. 87

Ho'oponopono Links 88

Mantras & Prayers 89

Introduction

As hard as I try I can't remember when or how I first heard of Ho'oponopono. That I can't remember is even more puzzling to me when I look at its tremendous effect on every part of my life.

Ho'oponopono (*Ho Oh Pono Pono*) roughly translated as *"to make right"*, *"to correct"*, is an ancient transformational and healing technique originating in Hawaii. Its simple message of 100% responsibility, repentance, and gratitude has been changing the lives of all it touches. Originally practiced by the native Hawaiians, Ho'oponopono was primarily a group based ceremony, used to solve community based problems and disputes. It has ties and similarities to many indigenous shamanic practices found throughout the world.

The Ancient Hawaiians understood the power of the mind. Centuries before mainstream science they identified the distinction between the **Conscious**, **Subconscious**, and **Super-Conscious Minds**, and the part they play in forming our present day circumstances.

This knowledge was considered so important that they built their whole belief system; **Huna** (*The Secret*) around it...

Huna's main focus was on resolving community disputes and problems. They discovered the best way to accomplish this was by understanding and controlling the power of the *Subconscious Mind*. The Ho'oponopono process was one of the most powerful tools they had in achieving this. It was used to clean and reset the mind, leaving it free and open to the positive influences that are constantly being sent to it from **the Divine Universal Consciousness.**

As with all ancient tribal practices its use has declined dramatically over the last few decades, social changes and modernity made it increasingly difficult to practice. It wasn't until the late 1970s that the late Morrnah Simeona took Ho'oponopono and updated it to reflect the demands of the modern world. No longer needing a collective the technique could now be practiced individually.

She called the new 12 step process; *Self-I-Dentity Through Ho'oponopono* (SITH), and established *The Foundation of 'I'* in Hawaii to bring the updated version to the world's attention-

"The main purpose of this process is to discover the Divinity within oneself. The Ho'oponopono is a profound gift which allows one to develop a working relationship with the Divinity within and learn to ask that in each moment, our errors in thought, word, deed or action be cleansed. The process is essentially about freedom, complete freedom from the past"- Morrnah Simeona (1913-1992). [1]

Morrnah was so respected and loved for her work with Ho'oponopono that in 1983 she was made a *"National Living Treasure"* by the Hawaiian people.

Since then Ho'oponopono has been quietly but steadily spreading around the globe, gathering rave reviews and devotees as it goes.

So what exactly is Ho'oponopono? Is it really so easy? Does it work? Why does it work? How do you do it? What can it do for me?

This book will answer these questions and many more, examining its origins, development, and the philosophy that underpins it. It will provide you with all the knowledge and information you need, guiding you through the Ho'oponopono process step by step with sample mantras so you can begin practising right away. We'll look at why this deceptively easy, but extremely powerful process, is changing the lives of millions around the globe.

And show you how it can change yours too...

CHAPTER 1

What is Ho'oponopono? Ho'oponopono & Universal Law

Ho'oponopono is an extremely simple, transformative, and healing process which is used by individuals to solve problems in their lives. The technique is used to clear, heal, and open the mind, freeing the practioner from negative *past memories* and *unconscious programmes*.

I like to call it the *"Karma Cruncher"*

It is based on the principle that each of us carries with us many lifetimes of karmic debt and other negative emotional baggage in the form of conscious, but mainly unconscious memories. It is to these memories that the subconscious mind turns to when making its decisions and judgments, and it is these memories that create the reality and circumstances we see around us in our lives.

By employing the Ho'oponopono technique to petition a higher spiritual power individuals can resolve these issues. Freeing them to live the rest of their time on earth empowered, living lives guided by inspiration, not fear and guilt.

The petition is carried out in the form of a mantra and is a personal request for forgiveness to God- *The Source, Universal Mind, The Void,*

Divine Intelligence, Universal Consciousness, (whatever you choose to call it), for reconciliation and forgiveness for past actions and deeds.

By acknowledging and accepting responsibility for our past actions we are able to free ourselves of their effects. The more you clean the more you free yourself to follow your true path and reach your full potential.

The ultimate aim of the Ho'oponopono practitioner is to erase (*clean*) his/her subconscious mind in order to reach a *State of Zero*. In this state, which Dr Hew Len calls *"Zero Limits"*- we are limitless, memory free, resistant free, and open to inspirational thoughts flowing down from Divine Intelligence through our super-conscious minds. Our goal is to negate our past actions through repentance and clear any conscious or subconscious resistance (blocks) we might have to new ideas, possibilities, and paths.

"What you resist persists". Carl Jung, (1875-1961) [2]

Ho'oponopono practice not only cleans and clears our minds and improves our receptivity, it also gives us a direct connection to the *greatest source* of power, wisdom, and knowledge imaginable **The Universal Mind.** It is from this power that *all* of mankind's' greatest achievements and ideas have sprung-

"The Universal Mind contains all knowledge. It is the potential ultimate of all things. To it, all things are possible". Ernest Holmes, (1887-1960) [3]

Ho'oponopono is **not a religion**. It is an intensely personal spiritual practice that individuals can use to communicate with their inner selves and with the source of their very existence. It has roots in animistic belief systems, believing that all living and material things are connected, that the Earth *(Gaia)* itself is a living spiritual conscious being.

In Ho'oponopono there are no *priests* or *gurus*, no *masters* or *leaders,* and no paths to follow. It needs no one but yourself, knows no boundaries, and can be practised, by anyone, anytime, anywhere.

Whatever spiritual path you follow Ho'oponopono is a wonderful tool. Some have even described its results as miraculous, but in truth Ho'oponopono is based on and subject to the **12 Universal Laws** and to fully understand the process we must look at it in the context of these laws:

1. Law of Divine Oneness.

2. Law of Vibration.

3. Law of Action.

4. Law of Correspondence.

5. Law of Cause & Effect.

6. Law of Compensation.

7. Law of Attraction.

8. Law of Perpetual Transmutation Energy.

9. Law of Relativity.

10. Law of Polarity.

11. Law of Rhythm.

12. Law of Gender.

The Law of Oneness: This is the Law that binds us together. It states that *everything* and everyone in the Universe is *connected.* We all come from the same **Divine Source-**

"A human being is part of the whole, called by us 'Universe'; a

part limited in time and space. He experiences himself, his thoughts and feelings as something separated from the rest—a kind of optical delusion of his consciousness. This delusion is a kind of prison for us, restricting us to our personal desires and to affection for a few persons nearest us. Our task must be to free ourselves from this prison."- Albert Einstein, (1879-1955) [4]

Every thought or action we have ever had, either positive or negative, **affects everyone**. If we hurt others we hurt ourselves. Nothing is separate. Separation is just an illusion we allow ourselves in order to experience what it feels like to be away from The Source-

"Quantum Physics reveals thus reveals a basic oneness of the universe" - Erwin Shrodinger, (1887-1961) [5]

The Law of Vibration: Nothing rests, everything moves, everything vibrates. Everything in the Universe is but a vibration-

"Everything changes and nothing stands still"- Plato, (427-347bc) [6]

The Physical and Spiritual worlds and everything in them- every thought, every emotion, every atom has its own unique vibration. For us to progress spiritually we only have to raise our vibration. Unconditional love is the *highest* emotional vibration and hate the *lowest*.

Modern Scientific research in Quantum Physics has proven that the Universe and everything in it is pure energy vibrating at different frequencies-

"The day science begins to study non-physical phenomena, it will make more progress in one decade than in all the previous centuries of its existence. To understand the true nature of the universe, one must think it terms of energy, frequency and vibration"- Nikola Tesla, (1856-1943) [7]

Here on earth the highest vibration we can attain is that which they call *enlightenment*.

The Law of Action: Works in tandem with *the Law of Attraction*. Thoughts alone are not sufficient when manifesting. They must be accompanied with corresponding actions.

Knowledge alone is not power. You can't just sit at home and pray for things to change, or wait for the right conditions before you act. You have to take the first steps on faith alone and if you do *The Universe* will do the rest...

The Law of Correspondence: *"As within so without"*. This law underpins the belief that in order to change the world around us we must first change ourselves. The idea that the world we live in is a manifestation of our internal thoughts and feelings is a fundamental belief in Ho'oponopono.

"Life is a mirror and will reflect back to the thinker what he thinks into it" – Ernest Holmes [8]

Think of it like this. We really only have complete control over one thing in our lives- **our thoughts.**

No-one can tell us what to think or feel!

If we can *control* what we think, we can *create* the reality we desire.

Unfortunately most of us have no idea what we are thinking most of the time. Try this simple test to find out what vibration you're really sending out into the Universe-

Monitor every thought you have for the next hour. If it is a negative thought- judgment, anger, frustration, anger, anxiety, fear etc then discard it as quickly as you recognise it.

If it is a positive thought- joy, excitement, happiness, contentment, admiration, love, compassion.. then nurture it, hold it and the associated feelings with you as long as you can.

All you have to do to pass the test is have more positive thoughts than negative- 51% will do to start. If you're feeling really brave try it for a whole day...

The Law of Cause and Effect: Nothing happens by chance. Every action or thought has an equal or opposite reaction. Tied in with the *Law of Oneness* this law again enforces why we must take **full responsibility** for the effects we see in our lives, because we at some point caused them.

"As you give out you shall receive" Michelangelo, (1475-1564) [9]

The Law of Compensation: This is a world of balance and harmony. The Universe is both self organising and self correcting, and no good deed is left unrewarded.

This law ensures that we are rewarded for any past acts of kindness or love, that at the time we may not have received. This compensation can come to us in *this life* or in *the next*. It comes in many forms; gifts, money, friendships, health, talent...

The Law of Attraction: *"Like attracts like"*. Whatever you focus your thoughts and energy on that is what you will attract, either good or bad.

Many of you will have heard of the Law of Attraction, made famous in books such as *"The Secret"* . The process has millions of practitioners throughout the world, and there are many similarities between the Law of Attraction technique and the Ho'oponopono process. Many of the core beliefs such as reincarnation, Divine Intelligence and the ability to co-create are the same.

But there are also fundamental differences Ho'oponopono's focus on *100% personal responsibility* for our actions, and circumstances, and its emphasis on *surrender* to The Divine's will to decide what is best, is significantly different than Law of Attraction's, with its intense focus on specific visualization.

As I mentioned before, *Like attracts Like.* The Universe sends us what we think and feel and Law of Attraction practitioners use this to facilitate their results.

And it does work in a limited way, albeit sporadically.

But it is only part of the process...

Using visualization, lists, and other tools, they focus entirely on the outcome of the petition. This technique puts the *conscious mind* in the driving seat, as it is used to generate the required emotion/vibration. It is no secret that the conscious mind and its ego are extremely difficult to control. When focusing on a future outcome or ideal it is very easy to start generating counter-productive negative emotions such as impatience, frustration and anxiety. Sending these types of emotions out into the Universe can only exasperate the initial problem.

The Ho'oponopono process takes a far different and simpler approach. In Ho'oponopono we only have to identify the areas in our life that we'd like to address and send a petition to The Divine for redemption and cleansing.

The rest of the process is left to the vastly superior perspective and wisdom of the *Universal Mind* to decide the best outcome.

I do use visualizations in my Ho'oponopono practice, as it assists me to create the emotions I feel are necessary when petitioning, but I try not to tie them to a specific request or outcome. I deliberately avoid using detailed pre-visualisations of what I request. I don't try to manipulate the world with sheer force of will. Importantly I avoid having any preconceived ideas of the outcome of my petition or how it will manifest.

Ho'oponopono practice is as much about enjoying the journey as it is about manifesting results- plus I like surprises...

My only aim is to leave a *clean void* for The Divine to fill as it sees fit- trusting in it with its infinite knowledge and wisdom, to know what is best for me and all concerned.

Law of Perpetual Transmutation of Energy: This little known law is at the very core of Ho'oponopono. It states that each of us has the ability to change the circumstances of our lives.

Higher vibrations *always* have the power to *consume* and *transmute* lower vibrations. We are never trapped no matter the circumstances of our lives. The Universe always allows us the opportunity to grow and evolve and is constantly giving us opportunities to do so. All we have to do is raise our vibration and take action.

"The most important decision we make is whether we believe we live in a friendly or hostile universe" Albert Einstein , (1879-1955) [10]

If you are on the right path, if you face each day with love and compassion then *The Divine* will give you all the help and assistance you need. Be sure of that.

The Law of Relativity: All things are relative. Nothing is good or bad unless we make it so-

It just is...

Nothing in our lives has any meaning unless it relates to us. The lessons we set ourselves in this life are based around this law. How could we empathise with someone who has lost a child if we had never known loss ourselves? How could we comfort a friend with a broken heart if we hadn't experienced the same?

Of course we don't experience all these losses/lessons in this lifetime alone that would be overwhelming. We do though carry the memories of our previous lives experiences with us as we progress.

This is why you can feel such strong empathy, even grief, for someone who has lost a child. For though you might not have lost one yourself in this life, you can be pretty sure you have suffered this tragedy yourself in one of your past incarnations...

The Law of Polarity: This law states that everything that exists has an opposite- *Love* and *hate, dark* and *light, success* and *failure, happiness* and *sadness,* one cannot exist without the other.

As all things in The Universe are *One* (the same), then nothing can be different-hot is the same as cold, pain the same as pleasure just at different ends of the spectrum. It is only our perception of them that changes.

By allowing us to experience both sides, polarity creates balance and harmony in the universe, and allows us to fully experience, and appreciate our experiences here on Earth-

"As above so below." Hermes Trismegistus (Pseud) [11]

Law of Rhythm: Everything in the Universe vibrates and moves in certain rhythms.

"Everything has its tides; all things rise and fall; the pendulum-swing manifests in everything; the measure of the swing to the right is the measure of the swing to the left; rhythm compensates."- The Kybalion [12]

These rhythms form the cycles and patterns we see in our lives; the rise and fall of our nations and economies, *"The Circle of Life"* as they call it in the movie *"The Lion King"*.

By remembering that the pendulum always swings back, we can view the events in our lives in a more balanced way.

"To everything there is a season, a time for every purpose under heaven" Ecclesiastes 3:1 [13]

Law of Gender: There are **two parts** to this law-

The First states that everything in nature has a masculine and feminine, *Ying* and *Yang*. Both are vital and equally important. Again the goal is to allow us to experience both, and to find a balance between them.

The Second governs creation in the physical world and states that everything has a gestation period, even thoughts. Nothing in this world happens instantly. It takes nine months for a baby to be born. An oak seed will take a little longer. When we have a thought we plant a seed in the Universe. And like everything in nature only by nurturing that seed will we see it grow.

Most people give up if they don't see instant results. Don't give up on your dreams and goals. Be assured that they are growing, and manifesting their way into your life. All you have to do is nurture them, and try to remember-

"Everything comes to you in the right moment, be patient". - [anon]

One final law that we should be aware when creating is **The Law of Probability** which is a sub-law to The Law of Attraction-

When we shift from our old reality to the new one it is done gradually, in small, incremental, dimensional shifts. The Universe will begin to synchronise with whatever we already have in our lives. If you are living in a shack, destitute, with no education or prospects, you won't suddenly find yourself in a high powered career, living in a penthouse.

That would be **improbable.**

But you may find that job that will help you move into a better house. Unexpectedly you might discover that your kids qualify for a free scholarship. Things will improve and keep improving, until one day you just might find yourself in that penthouse. If that's what you *really* want...

You have to ask yourself what is the likelihood of me winning the lotto?

Slim to none.

What about if you haven't even bought a ticket? What is the probability now?

None...

The same goes with health issues. Though we choose to live in an age of tremendous medical advancements, some things are still impossible. You are not suddenly going to re-grow a limb. We must work within the limits of our times. Of course these boundaries will change and expand, as mankind evolves and progresses.

"Nothing endures but change."- Heraclitus, (535-475bc) [14]

Until then we have to work with the forces and laws that govern this physical plane.

CHAPTER 2

Ho'oponopono Philosophy

As well as conforming to Universal Law some of the other core beliefs that underpin the Ho'oponopono's process are-

A Universal Mind or Consciousness

The belief in some form of *Universal Mind* or *Divine Consciousness* is fundamental in the majority of the world's religions and spiritual teachings, and Ho'oponopono is no exception. The nature of this God consciousness and its relationship with us is crucial in understanding how and why the Ho'oponopono process works.

Whether it is called; *God, Allah, Brahman, Yahweh, The Divine, Universal Mind or Universal Consciousness-* a creator who is Omnipotent (*all powerful*), Omniscient (*all knowing*), Omnipresent (*present everywhere at the same time*), Omnificent (*all creating*), is central in many religions and spiritual teachings.

But unlike the Christian concept of God as a separate supreme deity who rules and holds moral authority over us. A higher power outside ourselves, superior to us. One that we have to worship and beg if we desire change in our lives. In Ho'oponopono philosophy there is **no separation** or difference between us and our creator. We are a complete and identical part of the all, made in the exact image of God, *a chip off the old block.*

"Each of us is a microcosm, or fractal, of the entire universe. The entire universe rests within the centre of your Being. So in a sense we

are all One with the universe. But in the sense that the entire universe is manifest within us, just as we are manifest within it. We are all intricately connected. In fact, that connectedness is so intricately woven, that it can appear as one, just like a tapestry appears as one piece, yet there are many threads that make up the tapestry. So in a sense, we are One.. "- Greg Calise [15]

The Universal Mind is *all there is* and we are part of that all and as such we hold all the same powers as it does-

"There is no need for temples, no need for complicated philosophies. My brain and my heart are my temples; My philosophy is kindness" - The Dalia Lama [16]

"The Kingdom of God is With You"- Jesus [17]

There is *no out there*...your true self, your true divinity lies dormant and waiting within you.

Even Buddha was amused when he discovered the illusion-

"Bodhidharma laughed for seven days when he became enlightened - nonstop. His friends became very worried; they thought he had gone insane. They asked him, "What is the matter? Why are you laughing?"

He said, "I am laughing because now I see the whole ridiculousness of my search. I have been searching for **lives together for the truth, and it has always been within me.**

What I was searching for was in the seeker himself. I was looking everywhere and it was within me. I was running hither and thither and there was no need to run anywhere. I could have just calmed myself down, and it was mine. It has always been mine. From the very beginning it was within me. It is my innermost being, my very being. There is no need to go anywhere. There is no need to do anything. Just close your eyes and look within, and the kingdom of God is yours. Hence, I cannot stop laughing. " - Buddha [18]

The abiding message from great teachers throughout the ages is that if we want to connect with God then we only have to look within ourselves. All the answers, all the power lies dormant in each one us, waiting for us to wake up and realise our true divinity.

If we desire to change something in our lives, then that change already exists within us. There is no-one outside ourselves to whom we can beg or implore for help, no-one to blame except ourselves. Everything that we want, need, and desire already exists in The Universe all we have to do ask-

"Ask and you shall receive, seek and you shall find, knock and the door will be opened for you" - Matthew 7.7-11 [19]

It is not only in religious and spiritual teachings that we discover evidence of a great source of power and inspiration- evidence of the connectedness of the Universe and all it contains. Throughout history the world's political and business leaders, the world's greatest scientific minds, our innovators, our artistic geniuses all attest to a power greater than themselves. A source of knowledge and wisdom that when tapped into provides them with insight and inspiration-

"God's inner presence, beyond a doubt, constitutes the inspiration of men of genius" - Eugène Delacroix, (1798-1863) [20]

"The supreme God exists necessarily, and by the same necessity He exists always and everywhere"- Sir Isaac Newton, (1643-1727) [21]

"Everyone who is seriously involved in the pursuit of science becomes convinced that a spirit is manifest in the laws of the Universe-a spirit vastly superior to that of man, and one in the face of which we with our modest powers must feel humble. To which we are all connected to part of and equal to.." Albert Einstein [22]

"Part of and equal to"! Here is a scientist, a man considered to be one of the greatest minds of his or any other generation, telling us directly that we and everything else in the Universe are *connected to* and *equal to* what is more commonly known as God!

We are *in God* and God *is in us*, each and every one of us is a unique expression of God's Consciousness. Throughout the history of mankind great spiritual and metaphysical teachers, scientists and philosophers have told us that the answers we are seeking are within-

"Nothing can bring you peace but yourself"- Ralph Waldo Emerson [23]

We are *Divine Beings* and as such we have access to all of the wisdom and knowledge of The Divine, and all the same powers of creation and manifestation. We are in everything and everything is in us- all the happiness, joy, love, money, success we have dreamed of already exists in the Universe for our thinking about it made it so-

"Everything you can imagine is real."- Pablo Picasso, (1881-1973) [24]

The only reason that the things we desire in our lives are not present is because they are at a different vibrational level than we are. If we wish to attract change all we have to do is match our frequency to it and it will naturally and effortlessly work itself into our lives-

"Everything is energy and that's all there is to it. Match the frequency of the reality you want and you cannot help but get that reality. It can be no other way. This is not philosophy. This is physics"- Darryl Anka (Bashar) [25]

100% Responsibility

The Ho'oponopono technique is very easy to learn. What is not so easy is that in order to practice effectively, you first have to accept that you are 100% responsible for the world and everything you see and experience in it.

I mean everything!

Everybody, every act or reaction, whether good or bad, all the wars, all the hate and injustice in the world, all the suffering was created by you and you alone. The world around you in all its majesty and misery, all of it, is a *direct result of your thoughts.*

Co-creation - *Your thoughts shape your reality...*

The circumstances of your life are a mirror of the inner you. As stated in the Law of Attraction; *Like attracts Like*, and you attract the people and circumstances that reflect what you are, and where you are in your spiritual journey.

If the universe is brought down to the energetic or vibrational level, vibrations of a similar frequency are attracted to each other, and those not compatible to our current vibrational frequency are repelled. Simply put thinking good/positive thoughts raises our vibration and bad/negative thoughts lower it.

This concept is not new. It is a long held belief in many metaphysical circles that we are here on earth with free will, and as gods with the power to co-create.

The popularity of The Law of Attraction and success of books such as "*The Secret*" has proven how widespread these ideas have become.

The core of these beliefs is that your thoughts create your reality, and by controlling and focusing what you think, you can shape circumstances and events in your life-

Your thoughts, **conscious and unconscious** send a signal (a vibration) out to the Universal Consciousness and we attract back exactly what we impress on it. If we are constantly sending out negative thoughts and emotions then this is what we will attract back-

"A man is but the product of his thoughts what he thinks, he becomes."
- Mahatma Gandhi, (1869-1948) [26]

So if your thoughts create your reality...What are you thinking about today?

Now like me you're probably asking yourself *why*, if I have free will and the power to create anything, would I create a world around me full of hate, violence, and fear?

Why would I put myself in hardship, in poverty, in ill health?

The simple answer to that is because you didn't do it deliberately.

It is important to note that *all our thoughts*, conscious and unconscious contribute to the vibration we send out, but it is the unconscious mind that wields the most influence on our daily realities.

Most of us spend the majority of our lives running on pre-conditioned programs stored in our subconscious minds. And unless we are actively directing, monitoring, and filtering what our minds are thinking; through prayer, meditation, visualisation, contemplation, mantras, and other spiritual and metaphysical practices, then our subconscious mind will use these programs to form our realities for us.

"Only one millionth of what our eyes see, our ears hear, and our other senses inform us about appears in our consciousness." - Tor Nørretranders, "The User Illusion" [27]

In the absence of a captain your ship has been sailing itself.

The majority of our decisions and actions in our daily lives are based on *past experiences* and *old memories* replaying-

What happened the last time I did this? What was the result?

It is widely accepted that past traumatic events in a person's life can cause significant reactions and major personality changes for many years after the event. Memories that we have repressed play an even bigger role in shaping our lives. Mainstream therapy is focused on re-calling these memories and facing up to them as a form of resolution. It is not difficult to see how these past experiences help shape and form our lives and attitudes today. How you remember the past can dictate your present day view of the world-

That is undeniable...

But can these memories shape our very reality?

Reincarnation

Ho'oponopono takes this idea one giant leap further, suggesting that we not only carry with us all the memories and experiences of **this life**, but also those from all our **past lives** as well!

Ho'oponopono practitioners believe that we are all eternal, spiritual beings, incarnating here on earth in physical form in order to learn and progress spiritually.

This can take many lifetimes to achieve, and we do it by learning to overcome obstacles in this life in a loving and compassionate manner. Each incarnation is presented to us as an opportunity to evolve spiritu-ally, the latest in a long line of lives stretching back many eons-

"I did not begin when I was born, nor when I was conceived. I have been growing, developing, through incalculable myriads of millenni-ums. All my previous selves have their voices, echoes, promptings in me. Oh, incalculable times again shall I be born." - Jack London, (1876-1916) [28]

"There is no death. How can there be death if everything is part of the Godhead? The soul never dies and the body is never really alive."-Isaac Bashevis Singer, (1902-1991) [29]

Karma

As discussed in the previous chapter our lives here are governed by certain immutable Universal Laws. One these is The Law of Correspondence, sometimes referred to as *The Great Law*, more commonly known as *Karma*.

We don't start over with a clean slate every time we begin a new life. That would lead no-where, we arrive here with all the knowledge, wisdom, and love for which we have struggled and, worked so hard to earn.

Unfortunately, as well as all the good we have done, the lessons we have learned, and the progress we have made, we also bring with us all the garbage- the karmic debt, the hate, the fear, the guilt, and the prejudices we have accumulated over many difficult and challenging lifetimes.

Our entire lives' experiences, past and present, are stored forever in our *subconscious minds*. Every deed, thought, and act we have ever carried out, either in this life, or any of our past lives has been recorded for all time. This information is recorded and stored in our subconscious mind in the form of memories. The subconscious mind if undirected then uses that information to dictate our thoughts, feelings and actions in this lifetime. It is these memories that are being used to create our own individual realities.

In order for us to move on we are continually presented with opportunities to clear karmic debt. Unfortunately instead of resolving the problem we frequently get *stuck in a loop*. Many of us find ourselves repeating the *same mistakes* over and over again, finding ourselves in the same situations repeatedly as if we were deliberately punishing ourselves for some forgotten guilty act.

Well perhaps we are...

No Expectations

This is a difficult one, unlike many spiritual and metaphysical techniques in Ho'oponopono we don't focus on attracting or creating a specific ideal. The aim is to reach a state of openness/receptivity, to be clean and clear, in order to receive what The Divine deems best for us. This is not to say that we can't work on specific needs we identify in our lives. It is our job to recognise and target the problem areas and free ourselves from their influences, but how the problem or issue is resolved is entirely up to The Divine with its vastly broader perspective of the situation.

Have *no expectations* on the outcome of the petition is very easy to say... It is our natural human state to wonder, to plan and scheme, to dream. But for Ho'oponopono to work effectively we have to have faith, more than faith, we have to **know** that The Divine will provide the most elegant and suitable solution to our petition.

Once we accept that we are not capable of conceiving how or when something will happen, the rest will occur naturally, and work out to everyone's satisfaction. By doing this we free ourselves from constant longing, and open ourselves to outcomes we could never even imagine.

Spiritual Evolution

As we discussed earlier our goal here on Earth in this life is to grow and evolve spiritually ultimately working our way back from whence we came many eons ago. To assist us in our quest as we go through our lives we will be presented with obstacles and difficulties. It matters not if we fail in these challenges- it is how we respond to these difficulties that is important.

Each of us has the freedom to choose how we think, feel and ultimately act. What we think is the one thing that we do have complete control over in our lives-

No-one can tell you what to think.

When we are faced with an issue or circumstance in our life we have only two choices-

We can choose to address the problem in a loving and compassionate manner, one which ultimately satisfies all parties involved as much as it can.

Or we can choose to react with our basest of emotions- fear, prejudice, jealousy and hate.

The choice is ours alone-

"We cannot choose our external circumstances, but we can always choose how we respond to them."- Epictetus, (55–135 C.E.) [30]

«Consciousness cannot initiate an action, but it can decide that it should be carried out.» - Tor Nørretranders, "The User Illusion" [31]

What usually happens when we are faced with these often difficult decisions and dilemmas is that we avoid responsibility and again revert back to auto pilot. We allow our *subconscious mind to decide* the best course of action and it in turn has only past memories and pre-programming to rely on when determining its course of action.

The subconscious mind sends us exactly what we expect in life, it is a perfect reflection of the inner you. You might project a confident front to the world, but if inside you are full of doubt and fear, if negativity is your dominant emotion then that will be reflected in your life's circumstances today.

It is crucial to remember that your subconscious mind is **subjective.** It makes no judgments good or bad, We are here on Earth with free will and it can only give us what we ask for, or in our absence what it thinks we want.

Whatever we focus our attention (thoughts) on either consciously or unconsciously, then that is the reality that your subconscious mind will create for you.

"Match the frequency of the reality you want and you cannot help but get that reality."-Bashar [32]

There is no hiding place from your own mind...

That life seems to be constantly repeating itself is a common theme for a lot of people. This is because your subconscious mind prefers the status quo, it associates change with risk. The end result is usually a lifetime spent worrying needlessly, and repeatedly facing the same problems and issues over and over again, paralysed with doubt and fear.

Until we overcome these challenges and learn the lessons from them, then it is impossible for us to progress spiritually.

The Universe is a patient and benevolent place and it loves us so much that it constantly presents us with opportunities to address and face up to our fears and past mistakes without ever taking away our right to *free will.*

Earth School

Earth is the perfect place for us to learn, to grow, to evolve. We bravely choose to enter this world of duality and separation, virtually blind, with our perspectives narrowed considerably.

Why? Because these are the perfect conditions for the task at hand.

How could we take life seriously if we knew our real magnificence, our true selves? The knowledge that we are eternal beings, alone, would make a mockery of much of the drama and pain in the world.

Synchronicity

We've all experienced moments in our lives that seem to defy explanation, moments that can't be explained. Wonderful times when everything falls into place and the right people appear in your life exactly when they are needed. Something we recognise as more than pure luck or coincidence...

It was Carl Jung who first coined the term *"Synchronicity"*. He spent over 20 years of his life studying this phenomenon before publishing his thoughts-

In Jung's view synchronistic events occur because we live in an "Synchronistic Universe"-

"A synchronistic universe balances and complements the mechanistic world of linear causality with a realm that is outside of space, time and causality. In a synchronicity, two heterogeneous world-systems, the causal and acausal, interlock and interpenetrate each other for a moment in time, which is both an expression of while creating in the field an aspect of our wholeness to manifest. The synchronistic universe is beginning-less in that we are participating in its creation right now, which is why Jung calls it "an act of creation in time."- Paul Levy [33]

Jung's Synchronistic Universe theory was a radical new way of thinking which embraced linear causality while simultaneously transcending it. He overcomes the issue of causality (cause & effect, action & re-action) by stating-

"Continuous creation is to be thought of not only as a series of successive acts of creation, but also as the eternal presence of the one creative act." - Carl Jung [34]

I liken it to God's *over-ride* button...

Synchronistic events are part of our new evolutionary consciousness. Constant *cleaning* through the Ho'oponopono process clears the space they need to manifest in our lives. If you stay vigilant and grateful for them you will experience more and more of their wonderful effects in your lives. Their presence is also a certain sign that you are on the right path, so keep doing what you're doing-

"Synchronicity is an inexplicable and profoundly meaningful coincidence that stirs the soul and offers a glimpse of one's destiny." - Phil Cousineau *"Coincidence or Destiny?"* [35]

Free Will

While we can't control what challenges life sends our way. Our lives are in no way pre-destined. Each of us is born with Free Will and the ability to make conscious choices-

But how free are we really if we spend the majority of our lives running on auto-pilot, or if our judgment has been clouded by the effects of past experiences?

We can only truly say that we have free will when we have *conscious awareness* and this can only be obtained by constant focus, awareness, and action on our part-

"Be vigilant; guard your mind against negative thoughts."- Gautama Buddha [36]

Duality

This is a world of duality, of *Ying* and *Yang. Light* and *Dark. Love* and *Hate-*

"There is no quality in this world that is not what it is merely by contrast. Nothing exists in itself"- Herman Melville (1819 -1891) [37]

We chose to live this life of opposites. How else could we appreciate the beauty and wonder surrounding us if we knew no want?

How could we experience *love* without *hate*, *health* without *illness?*

How would joy feel if we'd never known sadness?

These experiences are crucial and necessary in our spiritual evolution and it is how we react to these challenges that count in the long run.

In normal times these issues would eventually work themselves out over many lifetimes of karmic debt, but as many of us believe these are not normal times-

There is a lot of evidence suggesting that we are in a period of accelerated transition in our own and earth's spiritual advancement. It is my belief that the Ho'oponopono process has been gifted to us at this time to assist us in ours and the planet's ascension. The fact that you're reading this book and probably many others like it shows that you feel the shift as well.

Ho'oponopono is **not magic** you will still face many difficult challenges and decisions during your time here on Earth and only you can decide how you react to them. Ho'oponopono is just a tool, a technique, which allows us to connect with our higher consciousnesses, and with the only power that matters- **The Divine Universal Mind.**

In reality none of us need anything to accomplish this, we all have the capacity within us to connect to our higher selves, in fact none of us have ever been disconnected. The Ho'oponopono process is one of many valid ways to facilitate this communication. It provides us with a way of cleaning our minds of junk and preconditioned programs (I liken this to pressing the reset button on a computer).

Constant Ho'oponopono practice also gives us an opportunity to balance some of the negative karma we may have accumulated. But in my opinion the most powerful tool it gives us is the ability to dictate our life's circumstances by turning us into **"Conscious Creators"**- allowing us to face our future challenges *clean* and *clear,* and once again in full control of our own destinies... Not bogged down by lifetimes of fears and habits.

Chapter 3

How It Works. Who Are We Really? Activating the Process

How it works

Now that we know some of the philosophy and beliefs that underpin the process we can look at exactly how and why it works.

Ho'oponopono is a problem solving technique that allows individuals to solve problems in their lives instantly as they occur. These problems can range considerably; from health issues and personality flaws, to relationship and money problems. The Ho'oponopono process allows you to take back control of your life. No longer blowing through life randomly like a leaf in the wind it transforms you from an *Unconscious Creator* into a *Conscious Creator.*

The technique is used to resolve and clear past memories and old attitudes that have been influencing our lives negatively. By addressing, resolving, and clearing these issues you leave yourself open to synchronistic events, and inspirational thoughts, that are constantly trying to get through, creating a world around you that better suits your stage of spiritual evolvement in *this lifetime.*

To fully understand how Ho'oponopono works we have to ask ourselves one important question-

Who am I?

This might seem like an easy question but I mean the real you, the complete you, not the you created by your ego.

Not the you, you think you are!

One of the principle teachers of modern Ho'oponopono is *Dr Ihaleakala Hew Len Ph.D.*

Dr Hew Len studied under the founder of modern Ho'oponopono Morrnah Simeona for many years before becoming a teacher of the process himself at the *Foundation of 'I'* where he is currently the foundation's *Chairman Emeritus*.

After Morrnah's death in 1992, he continued to develop the process and has become probably the most well known and highly respected Ho'oponopono teacher in the world today.

In 2007, Dr Hew Len combined with best selling metaphysical author Joe Vitale, and together they published *'Zero Limits'* which has become a best seller around the world. The book outlines Dr Hew Len's fascinating philosophy, and an extraordinary account of the power of Ho'oponopono on a group of mentally ill prison patients. (See Chap 8) [38]

He explains the process as such- we as humans incarnated here on earth, are made up of three distinct parts-

1. **The Conscious mind**

2. **The Subconscious mind**

3. **The Super-Conscious mind**

These in turn are connected at all times with *Divine Intelligence*.

The *conscious* and *subconscious* mind together form the person we are in this physical world- our personality, our intellect, our ego.

The *super-conscious mind* and *Divine Intelligence* are also closely connected. Perfectly in tune with one another, they operate independently above. All four are equally important and together they form the incarnate being we are on Earth today.

After death the subconscious mind takes over the role of the conscious mind in this physical reality and the super-conscious mind then replaces the subconscious mind.

Though able to work seemingly independently from the others *all minds are always connected.* We are never separated from The Divine no matter what illusion we create around us- Never, not even when we are at or lowest, our meanest, our loneliest...

Our separation is only an illusion...

The conscious mind thinks that it is in charge, that it makes the decisions. It believes that it has the power to change things. It is utterly convinced that all it needs to succeed is hard work, dedication, and a bit of good luck.

The physical world we live and operate in is based on the fundamental principle that we can somehow shape events and circumstances in our lives, and the world around us, by sheer force of will. Instead of surrendering to the flow, and trusting the universe to decide what is best for us-

"If you are quiet enough, you will hear the flow of the universe. You will feel its rhythm. Go with this flow. Happiness lies ahead"- Buddha [39]

In reality the conscious mind is **not capable** of conceiving or generating ideas or actions on its own. It can **only perceive** what it experiences. Scientific research has proven that it is the subconscious mind that is responsible for the majority of our thinking-

"Man is not primarily conscious. Man is primarily non-conscious...
Our consciousness is our user illusion for ourselves and the world."-
Tor Nørretranders, "The User Illusion" [40]

Modern scientific research in this area is discovering that the subconscious mind is not only the depository of our past life memories, but that it decides on what action to take *before the conscious mind is even aware of it,* and it relies almost solely on the replaying of *past memories* and experiences stored in the *subconscious mind* to form its reality. It is in this state that most of us live out the majority of our lives, running on auto pilot with occasional flashes of inspiration-

"In fact, the unconscious may even decide what actions you will take: numerous studies show that actions that feel intentional are actually triggered before you are consciously aware of having made the decision to act. This is hard to believe, right?

However, the studies have been replicated many times. The implication is that the unconscious not only feeds a highly filtered view of the world to your conscious - it also feeds actions and decisions to it. The conscious can veto the decisions, but not initiate them!"- Tor Nørretranders, "The User Illusion" [41]

The *subconscious mind is hugely powerful and influential* in our lives although we barely notice. It controls every function of our bodies from our heartbeats and breathing, to our attitudes and responses. It never rests and without it we would be over-whelmed!

"Only one millionth of what our eyes see, our ears hear, and our other senses inform us about appears in our consciousness."- Tor Nørretranders, "The User Illusion" [42]

If you ever doubt the subconscious mind's control over you, ask yourself-

Who is it that is driving the car when your conscious mind begins to wander?

Sometimes I can drive for many miles with no recollection of having done so. As I forgot the illusion of being in control the real driver emerged. Each time we lose control of our thoughts through the fog of emotion; fear, anger, panic, or confusion, we give up the directorship of our lives.

That is not to say that the conscious mind is impotent, it still has a very important role to play. Influencing and controlling the information we send to the subconscious mind is **the most important task** you can ever accomplish in this life, controlling this flow of information (thoughts) is the secret to controlling your very reality.

«*Consciousness cannot initiate an action, but it can decide that it should be carried out.*" - Tor Nørretranders, "The User Illusion" [43]

We have the ability to use our conscious minds to impress on the subconscious the changes we want to make in our lives. **Complete consciousness** is the secret to controlling our mind. Only by being fully aware of what thoughts/vibrations we are projecting into the Universe can we hope to control them.

This is not an easy task. The conscious mind (our ego and intellect) is a very stubborn character; years of unconditioned and unguarded thinking have convinced it that it is the only "*real*" thing in the Universe. Our conscious mind thinks it runs the show, it believes it is always right and it allows its ego, judgements, and prejudices to colour its choices and decisions.

But in reality it has **no power** to create thoughts, ideas, or actions on its own. It is only used as an *avatar.*

The conscious mind's role is to allow us to experience the physical world vicariously, and it does this by using our five physical senses to form its view of reality-

"Through our eyes, the universe is perceiving itself. Through our ears, the universe is listening to its harmonies. We are the witnesses through which the universe becomes conscious of its glory, of its magnificence"- Alan Wilson Watts, (1915-1973) [44]

It is the subconscious mind that creates the world around us, and it relies almost exclusively on the replaying of pre-programs, and old memories to make its judgments-

"Man is not primarily conscious. Man is primarily non-conscious"-
Tor Nørretranders, "The User Illusion" [45]

The *Super-Conscious Mind is memory free* and is in direct contact with The Divine at all times. It is in tune with the flow of *The Source,* and it passes on these inspirations constantly. Unfortunately this doesn't happen as often as we'd like. The subconscious's prejudices and beliefs filters out those ideas that it fears, or cannot comprehend, relying instead on old thought patterns, programs, and past life memories.

The Ho'oponopono process is used to negate and transmute these memories. This in turn frees up space leaving us more receptive to inspirational thoughts and synchronistic events.

Dr Hew Len likens this process to *"cleaning"* the memory.

Activating the process

In order to impress on the subconscious mind the changes desired we have to focus the mind (our thoughts) on what it is we really want- not what we don't want. We have to be firm and sure on our goal, and then endeavour to generate the corresponding emotions (vibrations) requisite to attracting that vibrational state into our lives-

"Everything is here and now, but in various states of visibility and invisibility depending upon the frequency that you are operating on, and that means the belief system, the definitions that you buy into most strongly"- Bashar [46]

Transmutation

The Ho'oponopono mantra is used by the conscious mind to send a request to The Divine to cancel (*clean*) and transmute (*replace*) troublesome memories in order to free oneself from their influence.

This request passes into the subconscious mind which stirs and readies the targeted memories for **transmutation-** (*the action of changing or the state of being changed into another form*)

It is then passed to the super-conscious mind which reviews the problem from its own wider perspective. It makes any changes and adaptations it sees fit and finally it is passed on to Divine Intelligence for final approval.

After approval, and with any additional changes it deems necessary, The Divine sends healing transformational energy back down to the super-conscious mind into the conscious mind, and finally into the subconscious mind where it gently cleans out the problem memory.

This transmutation of lower energy into higher spiritual vibration brings us one step closer to what Dr Hew Len calls *"Zero Point"*. What Buddhists call *The Void*.

It is our natural state. In this state we are in tune, in balance, in harmony, and at one with The Universe. We liken it to being in the flow, open to all kinds of inspiration and synchronistic events. This is our **true state.** It is where we came from and where we will all return. Each of us bringing our own unique perspectives and experiences with us...

Ho'oponopono gives us the tools to reach that state of bliss *(zero)* whenever we want. It makes us our own therapist, healer, guru. It is only once this state has been achieved that we will begin to see tremendous changes in our lives.

An important difference in Ho'oponopono and a lot of other spiritual techniques is that we don't have to ask for something specific our only aim is to clear the way, the connection, to the limitless and eternal power of *The Universal Mind.* All we have to do then is await the inspiration that will flow down to us and act upon it.

Ask and you shall receive...

So now you know a little bit about the theory behind the process, it's time to start practising for yourself. The next chapter will show you how to identify problems correctly, and give you the only tools you will ever need to practice Ho'oponopono- *The Four Phrases.*

Chapter 4

Getting Started. The Four Phrases

The Four Phrases

I Love You...

I'm Sorry...

Please Forgive me...

Thank You...

These four ordinary phrases are the only tools you will ever need to practise Ho'oponopono. It is a deceptively simple technique, but don't be fooled, practising Ho'oponopono correctly is a full time occupation- call it a state of mind... And it can be very hard work!

The phrases are used to *"clean"* the problem memory, and together they form the foundation of all your future petition mantras sent to The Divine.

They are said silently to oneself, can be used in *any order* and repeated as much as you like. You don't have to clasp your hands or close your eyes as in prayer, but if this puts you in a better frame of mind then it's easy just to adapt your usual prayer routine to accommodate the phrases.

Identifying the problem

First we have to *identify the problem*. To do this we look at the situation we want to resolve and remind ourselves that it is not the person or situation that is the problem. It is our perception of them/it.

Then ask yourself what is it **in me** that is causing this problem?

Say for example I was having some minor health issues, in this case chest pain. After asking myself the question what is it in me that is causing this pain, this discomfort?

I conclude that perhaps I have not been taking care of my body as well as I should, that I've been neglecting it, taking it for granted, not appreciating its gifts.

Or maybe it's a symptom of some *karma* I've accumulated in a past life.

It matters little the initial cause of the pain. All that matters now is that we recognise and acknowledge the problem and make sincere attempts to rectify it.

After I've identified the problem I formulate my mantra in such a way as to accept **full responsibility** for it as below-

I Love You my body...

I'm Sorry for whatever I have done to cause you hurt, harm, pain, or discomfort...

Please forgive me...

Thank You...

Here is the same petition but embellished in order to create feeling.

I Love You my body...

I Love the strength and confidence you bring me. You have been a loyal and faithful companion to me on this physical journey...

I'm Sorry for whatever I have ever done to cause you pain and discomfort, in this life or any of other life...

I'm Sorry for neglecting you, and not appreciating your wonderful gifts...

Please Forgive me...

Thank You...

And the same petition formulated in a different way;

Thank You chest pain...

Thank You for bringing this problem to my attention, so I can address and resolve it...

I'm Sorry for whatever it is that I have done to cause you to manifest in my reality, to be part of my life...

Please Forgive me...

I Love You...

Let's have a closer look at the four phrases and how they can be adapted to any situation whether general or specific. They can be interchanged, used in **any order** and in any frequency. Below is an example of a simple non-specific general petition that I send first thing in the morning and before bed each night;

I Love You...

I'm Sorry for anything I have ever done to cause hurt, harm or pain to anyone, or anything, consciously or unconsciously, either by act or omission, in this life or any other...

Please Forgive me...

Thank You...

As you can see in this particular mantra we first express *love;*

Love for self, love for The Divine, and love for the opportunity to correct the problem.

I'm sorry shows our *contrition,* and acknowledges our role, and 100% responsibility in creating the problem.

Our plea for forgiveness *surrenders* us to the wisdom of a higher power to decide the best outcome.

And finally we show *gratitude* by giving thanks.

With Feeling or not?

Which bring us to one of the most common questions in Ho'oponopono... do you say the mantra with feeling or not?

Personally I prefer to embellish the wording of my mantras. I also use visualisation when petitioning. I feel it helps me generate the necessary positive emotions needed to properly activate and expose the troublesome memories.

This is where my interpretation of Ho'oponopono differs from that of Dr Hew Len; who states that **no feeling** either positive or negative is necessary when saying the petition. Before I explain further, I'd like to reiterate again that in Ho'oponopono there are no masters or leaders. There are no Popes or bishops. No gurus to guide you. It has no tenants, or rules to obey. No doctrines to follow, no wall to wail at-

There is only you...

You must trust in yourself to guide you- no-one else. The process is entirely open to your own interpretation. If it works for you then it's valid!

I'll explain why I use positive feelings when I petition.

To me both the *Physical and Spiritual Planes* rely primarily on feeling and emotion for communication, both with us, and with each other. In all I have read and researched about the spiritual world and its laws, it is clear that feelings and emotions, primarily love, are the *lingua franca* not words. Any communication I have ever had with The Divine has always come with strong feelings attached, so when I send up my cleaning petition it goes with as much positive emotion as I can muster.

I soon found whatever the issue was that I was addressing, the feelings that I needed to resolve it were usually the same; repentance, forgiveness, love, gratitude, joy, compassion...

How could it be possible to say the following petition to Mother Earth without feeling?

I love you Mother Gaia...

I love you for your beauty, your majesty, your inspiration, I love you for the warm sun on my face, the gentle breeze. I love you for your generosity and compassion, your unconditional love for us..

You provide us with all that we need; food, water, shelter, the very air that we breathe...

I'm sorry for anything I have ever done to cause you hurt or harm in this life or any other lifetime, consciously or unconsciously...

I'm sorry for neglecting you, for taking you for granted, for not appreciating your wonderful gifts...

Please forgive me...

Thank you...

Of course you can't have feelings for something you don't feel responsible for, or for an act that you can't remember. You might not know the cause of a particular problem but you can certainly see its effects in your life. In these cases it is the symptoms that we address, not the cause, as in this petition to solve a problem of low self esteem;

Thank you feelings of worthlessness and failure...

Thank you for coming to my attention so I can resolve you...

I'm sorry for whatever I have ever done to cause you to manifest in my reality, to be part of my life...

Please forgive me...

I love you...

Notice that I targeted the emotions caused by the memory, in this case feelings of low self esteem. Ho'oponopono practise is more concerned in dealing with the resulting memories and their continuing effects, rather than the incident that caused them. If you do want to know the details on your past life exploits in order to investigate further, there are many excellent hypno-therapists who specialise in past life or even between life regression.

From start to finish cleaning a problem in your life should only take **4 simple steps-**

Step 1: *Identify the problem*, by asking yourself what is it in me that is causing this problem?

Step 2: Using the four phrases *formulate your petition* mantra.

Step 3: *Send the mantra to The Divine* by internally repeating the phrases silently to yourself as and when the problem arises.

Repeat the mantra until the problem is resolved.

Step 4: *No Expectations;* not really a step but it is vitally important to remember to forgo any expectations on how, when, or even if, the petition will manifest...

One of the beautiful aspects of Ho'oponopono is that as soon as we have identified the problem, accepted responsibility for it, and sent our petition off to The Divine our job is done, finished completely. The rest of the process will happen automatically. Our conscious mind plays no further part in the process until it receives the healing energy back from the super -conscious.

As the Ho'oponopono process gets to work the world around you will quietly, without much fuss, begin to change. Circumstances in your life will slowly improve, as will your relationships with the people around you.

So now you have the tools to begin your journey. You have the *Four Phrases,* and know how to make a simple petition. It's nearly time to go get cleaning.

But before you do, in the next chapter I have covered some of the main issues and questions that arose when I first began using the process regularly.

Chapter 5

Ho'oponopono Practice & The Questions That Arise

So what can we clean?

Anything you desire...

Your personality, your health, your wealth, your circumstances. Other people, inanimate objects, animals, world affairs...

Absolutely anything! It may seem incredible that we as individuals sitting at home could have any influence on people and events around the world, but it is important to note here that it is not the person or circumstance that is the problem; it is *our perception* of them! It is a distorted image that we have created through a fog of fear and ignorance-

In order to change the world around us, first we have to change ourselves and our perception of it.

Inanimate Objects

One of the aspects of Ho'oponopono that surprises a lot of people is that fact that we can use the process to clean (improve) our relationships with inanimate objects; buildings, chairs, trees, rooms all have some level of consciousness. This is not as fantastic as it may sounds if we understand that we live in a vibrational universe-

"If you want to find the secrets of the universe, think in terms of energy, frequency and vibration."- Nikola Tesla [47]

Vibrational Universe

Everything in the Universe vibrates; the only difference is the rate at which it vibrates. It is this difference that creates the illusion of separateness we see in our worlds. In reality there is no difference between you, a tree or even the chair you're sitting in except the rate at which it vibrates!

"It followed from the special theory of relativity that mass and energy are both but different manifestations of the same thing"- Einstein [48]

You are a *vibrational being* in a *vibrational universe*. The world you see around you and everything in it is in a state of constant flux as all these different vibrations continually respond to or integrate with all other vibrations. This is where the concept of *Like Attracts Like* is based.

You are constantly vibrating and either repelling or attracting compatible vibrations. Today mainstream scientists such as particle physicist Dr John Hageln are discovering this invisible world in their work on unified field theories-

"Progress in theoretical physics during the past decade has led to a progressively more unified understanding of the laws of nature, culminating in the recent discovery of completely unified field theories based on the superstring. These theories identify a single universal, unified field at the basis of all forms and phenomena in the universe.

"At the same time, cutting-edge research in the field of neuroscience has revealed the existence of a 'unified field of consciousness'—a fourth major state of human consciousness, which is physiologically and subjectively distinct from waking, dreaming and deep sleep. In

this meditative state, a.k.a. Samadhi, the threefold structure of waking experience—the observer, the observed and the process of observation—are united in one indivisible wholeness of pure consciousness."- Dr John Hageln [49]

By practising Ho'oponopono regularly we can raise our vibrational energy and subsequently attract only vibratory energy fields (people, things, circumstances) commiserate with our new higher state. Lower baser vibratory fields will either be repelled or transmuted by our higher frequency.

If say a person was scheduled to enter your life in a negative way in order to help you resolve a karmic debt, maybe as a violent husband or a cheating wife. If we have already addressed and resolved this issue through Ho'oponopono practice then you would either not meet the person at all or if you did they would have no effect on you. For a violent husband to enter your life you both have to be on the same vibrational level; *aggression* and *cruelty* would be a similar level vibratory as say *weakness* and *fear,* so you would be attracted to each other. *Deceit* and *selfishness* would be attracted to *victim-ship* and *worthlessness.* If these emotions are no longer part of the inner you then you are no longer attractive to lower vibrations, in fact you will positively repel them.

The concept of higher vibration always overcoming lower is one of the founding principles of both the physical and spiritual world. Combine this with the inter-connectness of it all (even your chair) at a vibratory level and you can see why we can influence everything and anything, even so called inanimate objects such rocks or wood. Everything is vibration and connected at a vibratory level and every thought (vibration) you send out resonates and affects the all-

"Our entire biological system, the brain and the earth itself, work on the same frequencies" -Nikola Tesla [50]

What do I clean first?

As discussed above one of Ho'oponopono's core beliefs is that everything starts from within, and that in order to heal others we must first heal ourselves. With that in mind, I suggest starting with a small personal issue you might have with another person. It can be anyone, a colleague, a friend, a loved one. Try to ensure it is someone that you have regular contact with so you can monitor results.

Say the mantra as often as you can; *before* you see them, *during* contact with them and *afterwards* as well...

Try to have *no expectations* or preconceived ideas on the outcome of your efforts.

Here is an early petition I did to resolve an issue I had with a work colleague that you can use for your first petition;

I love you _____ *...*

I love you for teaching me patience, and restraint. About tolerance, and understanding...

I'm sorry for anything I have ever done to cause you hurt or harm...

I'm sorry if I have judged you, or offended you in any way...

Please forgive me...

Thank you...

I tend to concentrate my efforts on personal and family issues, such as ill health and relationship problems. At this stage of my development I find that Ho'oponopono works best with problems involving people's emotions. It is especially effective with relationship issues, for setting up synchronistic events, and generally smoothing your way in life.

When do I clean?

The mantra is used as problems arise, as you encounter them, or even before as a preventative measure. There are *no set times* or days that you set aside for Ho'oponopono practice. The mantra is said *silently and repeatedly* to yourself as you go about your daily life. This is why it is impractical to close your eyes, or clasp your hands in prayer.

Below are a couple of examples of simple preventative petitions, which I would use to smooth my way as I go about my daily life;

Say your manager has called you unexpectedly into a meeting, and he wants to meet you first thing after lunch.

First you *identify the problem*- Boss wants an unscheduled meeting with you, and this is causing you some anxiety.

Get to the cause of the issue by asking yourself what is it *in you* that is causing this problem of anxiety and fear?

Then formulate your mantra to suit the situation...

In this case, as I have no specific issue with my manager that I know of, I would concentrate on making sure my conscious and subconscious thoughts about the coming situation were positive ones.

I love you manager's name...

I love you for your kindness, your support, your generosity, and your friendship...

I'm sorry for anything I have ever done to cause you harm...

I'm sorry if I have judged you or not appreciated your support...

Please forgive me...

Thank you...

Say the mantra silently to yourself a few times *before* you go into the meeting- as many as you think the issue warrants. I try to visualise the person as I say the mantra, an easy one would be to visualise yourself and the person together smiling and laughing, or perhaps imagine yourself giving them a hug, anything to stimulate the correct emotions.

While you are in the meeting keep silently reciting the full mantra to yourself, or if this is impractible, a shortened version of *Thank you, I love you,* will do just as well.

Continue to say the mantra *after* the meeting has finished, again for as long as you judge it needs.

You are then free to move onto the next problem.

Notice that even if there is no particular issue with your boss, you're not expecting a rollicking and you're on good terms, we still use the mantra.

Again the mantra is extremely adaptable. I could have taken a completely different approach to the same situation. Instead of concentrating on my relationship with my boss to rectify the anxiety, I focus on myself as below;

*I love you **self belief** and **charisma**...*

I love the confidence you give me, the doors you open. The friends you help me meet. The tasks you help me accomplish...

I'm sorry for anything I have ever done consciously or unconsciously to block you and your wonderful gifts from my life...

Please forgive me...

Thank you...

Notice how I have identified the issue as a problem in me, not my boss. I examined the issue, and asked myself, what is it in me that is causing this problem?

Why is my subconscious creating this situation I am experiencing?

What lessons do I need to learn to resolve it?

In this case I know that I have some anxiety about the upcoming meeting, and as I have no known problems with my boss, I equate that with a lack of confidence in myself.

After I have identified the problem I then get to work cleaning the issue, ensuring that I go into the meeting empowered, and of course full of confidence.

And that is your goal with Ho'oponopono- to empower yourself. To free yourself of negative memories of regret, and guilt, allowing you to face the world a little bit *"cleaner"* each time you resolve a problem.

How often should I clean?

Let's be very clear Ho'oponopono practice is a full time occupation, almost *a state of mind.* Not when you are in the mood, or have some free time. Not on Sundays, not five times a day. It is demanding and it is constant.

Different problems require varying amounts of time. Keep cleaning until they are resolved. Most become ongoing, for example, a simple room, or house cleaning petition will probably be sent once or twice a day, but it could go on indefinitely. For health issues I generally clean until the symptoms disappear, and then top up regularly with a simple gratitude based mantra. World peace, or a cure for cancer, will take a bit more time and effort...

Please note; you can very quickly find yourself overwhelmed so choose your problems wisely- no-one expects you to cure the world's problems instantly. Each problem cleaned is a step in the right direction. Try to remember Dr Hew Len's words;

"Peace begins with me" [51]

Unless you are at peace with yourself you can't bring peace to others.

Do what you can...

Does it just happen or do I have to take action too?

Constant Ho'oponopono practice creates the environment, the circumstances, and the energy required for you to create the reality you desire, the rest is up to you. It provides you with the ladder, and each rung is a small step up your evolutionary climb. The more you clean the more you will find your life's possibilities open up. But at this stage that's all they are, **possibilities**...You still have to take the necessary steps to turn them into reality.

What results can I expect and how long will it take?

So finally we come to the important bit. If you remember back at the beginning of this chapter, I answered that we could clean anything, or anyone, we desired. Which is true as long as you take into account Universal Law?

You will have success with Ho'oponopono if you practise it correctly and regularly. I have yet to find someone who hasn't. If you focus your petitions, choose them wisely, and limit the amount you take on, you should see and feel results within a very short space of time. You will start to experience *gradual shifts* in your present reality. Things will start to go your way, you will experience more *synchronicity* in your life, and people will react to you more positively. The focus of your petition, the problem, will resolve, but again maybe not in the way you imagined.

It was these initial results that first grabbed my attention. I could not believe how quickly the process produced tangible results. I have tried many different spiritual techniques in the past and never once even after many months of effort have I achieved the results that Ho'oponopono gave me within days.

Chapter 6

Ho'oponopono and the Wider World

Ho'oponopono & Other People

Cleaning another person's problems is quite acceptable. There are no moral or free will dilemmas to consider. Each petition is considered by *The Divine* before any action is taken. I trust in its infinite knowledge and wisdom to formulate an outcome that is best for all parties concerned.

Again you have to use your discretion on which problems you choose to address. One of the first mistakes I did was to take on an elderly relative's health issues, in this case dementia. I quickly realised that realistically I was not going to cure him of this horrendous disease quickly, and as he is very elderly, I changed my petition from that focus, to one of alleviating his symptoms-

I Love you Uncle_____.

I love you for teaching me about compassion, about kindness, about sacrifice, and selflessness...

I'm sorry if I have neglected you, and not appreciated your wisdom, if I have taken you for granted...

I'm sorry for whatever I have done to cause you pain, or distress, or discomfort...

Please forgive me...

Thank You...

Cleaning community or world issues

As we covered previously we can clean on pretty much anything, or anyone, we desire. The Divine will answer each and every one of those petitions in the most suitable and elegant way.

At some point you will want to start cleaning on grander scale. You might have seen a news report, or read an article that moved you- a war, a conflict, a kidnapping, a missing child, a dying child...The world is full of injustices and atrocities. These are all things that move us and we are compelled to help.

And sometimes we do. We campaign, or protest, or donate, which helps for a while but usually we end up feeling helpless in the face of such overwhelming odds.

Ho'oponopono practice puts the power back in the hands of each and everyone one of us. Now **you can make a difference** to the world you see around you.

Something like a war is actually a relatively easy task to clean. Conflicts are usually based on fear and Ho'oponopono is excellent at resolving fear based situations between individuals, or groups. But in the case of a major conflict it is the sheer scale of the task that presents the problem. Major world events are often the result of **collective karma**. Resolving them has to be a group effort.

Individually we have incredible power, far more than we could ever imagine. Collectively we are unstoppable!

The world is slowly waking up to the fact that we are not helpless pawns, and that we can make a real difference to the world around us, if we come together with love and focus our attention on the problems surrounding us.

My lone petition below aimed at resolving the current *Russian/Ukrainian* crisis might seem futile, but I have faith that all around the world, thousands, maybe one day millions, of you are doing the same thing.

So I do what I can, and in the case below, I focus my petition on the fear between the two nations:

I love you Russia...

I love you Ukraine...

I love you for teaching the world about tolerance and understanding, for teaching us the value of patience and restraint...

I'm sorry for whatever I have done to cause this conflict between you, this fear and mistrust between your two nations. You deserve peace and prosperity and stability in your lives...

Please forgive me...

Thank you...

It's reasonable to expect that this problem will take a while to resolve so I move it to my daily petitions list and move on. I don't avoid any news on the subject after my petition has been made, but I don't go out of my way to find out either.

Something like a missing person is much more complicated. What if they are dead already? No amount of Ho'oponopono practice is going to bring them back. They could be missing indefinitely or never found at all...

Of course you will still try, as I do. Use your own judgement in these situations on both what to clean, and how long to keep cleaning. As you continue your practice you will soon learn what to problems to focus on and what to leave alone for now.

Am I alone?

The intensely individualistic nature of Ho'oponopono practice might leave you feeling alone. There is none of the support that many other religions and spiritual paths have. Sometimes it will feel as if you have the weight of the world on your shoulders.

It is always useful to *remember the principle of oneness* when attempting to understand any spiritual concept. Take comfort in the knowledge that we are in reality all parts of the whole, originating from and eventually returning to *The Divine Source* of all.

Remember that we have created this world of separation so we can experience what it is like to be far from *The Source* (The Divine).

Each of us is undergoing a very unique and personal and seemingly independent view of the universe but in reality we are *always connected*, both to our higher selves and the rest of creation. Every act or thought we have resonates throughout all creation. Whatever we do to improve ourselves, whenever we act in a loving manner, it all combines to improve the world around us.

Of course the opposite is true also, if you persist in seeing the world as a frightening, hostile, unfriendly place. Viewing it through eyes of fear and feelings of helplessness, then that is exactly what you will see and experience.

If you feel that the world is a safe, friendly place, full of helpful people and endless possibilities, then again, that is the world that will be reflected back to you.

"The most important decision we make is whether we believe we live in a friendly or hostile universe" - Albert Einstein [52]

So what world would you rather live in?

We have free will- it's your choice...

Although we live these lives under **the illusion of separation** we all live and experience the same world. World events and Earth changes affect us all, no matter how much cleaning we do. Humanity as a whole is *collectively evolving,* as are nations and ethnic groups, and we are all collectively responsible for our ancestors' actions.

Different groups evolve at different speeds, and in different ways, just as individuals do, and they collectively face different problems. The issues and obstacles facing the *African or Islamic* nations for example, will be vastly different from those that face the *Americans or Chinese.*

Again it is important to remember that there is no right or wrong way in either our individual or collective evolutions. All paths are valid. All roads will eventually lead us home.

We all get there in the end...

As we discussed in the previous chapter we can assist in this evolution, by collectively cleaning on our immediate world and the global issues that affect us all, such as wars and environmental concerns.

The petition below addresses the heartbreaking situation in North Korea, and is an issue close to my heart. The people there have *suffered long enough!*

I would be grateful if you could add it to your long term cleaning list.

I Love you North Korea, your people, and your land...

I love you for teaching the world about patience, compassion, and humanity...

I'm sorry for whatever I have done to cause this tyrannical regime to reign over you...

I'm sorry for whatever I have done to cause this black cloud of oppression to hang over your land...This brutal dictatorship...

Please forgive me...

Thank you...

Chapter 7

Success with Ho'oponopono

Does it work for everyone all of the time?

This is a very important question. Like myself many of you will have experienced the rush of immediate results when we first began practising Ho'oponopono regularly. In my case I then entered a period where I could see no discernable effects on the areas I was cleaning on. Initially I put this down to the built in gestation period we are subject to here on the physical plane. (see Law of Correspondence Chap 1) But then the doubts began to creep in.

Am I doing this right? Am I doing it enough? How much is enough? Does it really work?

It is at this point where you must not only practise Ho'oponopono you must begin to *master it!*

Most of the failures in Ho'oponopono come after that initial surge of success and there can only be one reason for that- complacency and laziness. Everyone knows what happens when we take our eye off the ball. Practising Ho'oponopono is no different-success requires focus and effort on our part, and the Divine will do the rest.

If we can get it right some of the time we can get it right all of the time. If the process itself worked initially then it must be something in us that has caused it to stop working. It is entirely normal for the initial surge of interest and enthusiasm to wear off in any new activity we undertake and Ho'oponopono practice is no exception.

When we first began to practise we were enthused full of energy, hope and excitement. Our *entire focus* was on Ho'oponopono and how to make it work. We read about Ho'oponopono, thought about it constantly and for a few days or weeks we lived and breathed it-

We were there... not just in thought but in feeling too.

Almost every spiritual philosophy stresses the importance of *mindfulness and awareness.* They stress the *importance of living in the now* and there is good reason for this.

If you fall into the trap of mindlessly repeating the phrases with no thought or focus then the brain will do what it does with all low concentration repetitive tasks- it will put them on auto-pilot. To the conscious mind this makes perfect sense as it can then return to the more important task of active thinking. Remember it thinks it runs the show.

Sleep walking around endlessly chanting mantras while allowing your conscious mind to do as it likes will get you nowhere. The secret to successful Ho'oponopono practice is that you have to be there! You have to be aware of the process, focused on your feelings, your thoughts, and your emotional state- at all times *monitoring* and *actively directing* your conscious mind. It is only your focus and awareness that can *compel your conscious mind* to action. This focus must be maintained at all times not only when you are practising. Try to be constantly aware of your emotions, thoughts and mood as you go about your day- make it your goal to maintain a higher ratio of positive thoughts than negative ones, try for at minimum of 51% positive thoughts over negative ones. If a negative thought surfaces in your mind quickly dismiss it with a Ho'oponopono mantra. Give it no real thought (focus) or attention. If it is positive nurture and embrace it, love it. Help it take root and grow in your mind and personality. You will be surprised how easy this becomes with practice.

Gratitude

One of the quickest ways of raising your vibration is through gratitude. Giving thanks for the blessings in your life is one of the most powerful tools you have in your armoury. As you go about your day, pay attention and look for things to be grateful for in your life- friends, health, family...you won't have to look far I promise. For all the good you find in your life send a simple *I Love.. Thank You*..mantra into The Universe. If you do then you'll receive more of it, it's that simple...

Remember your subconscious mind *sends you what it thinks you want* from the impressions (thoughts) you send to it.

Don't leave it to chance tell it exactly what you want and desire! Show passion and love for the beauty and abundance you already have and you can't fail to receive more of it.

Surrender & Trust

One of the major aspects of Ho'oponopono practice is **trust.** You have to have faith and trust in The Divine to decide what the best outcome is for all concerned. Surrendering to a higher power to decide the fate of my life was one of the most difficult aspects of Ho'oponopono for me. This surrender is a fundamental tenant of many religions and spiritual paths but it felt like giving up to me.

While I admire the faith of those devotees who can shut themselves in a monastery, or sit atop a mountain for decades, away from all the temptations and challenges of life. To me this seems to be contrary to the whole purpose of this physical existence...

We are here to experience life. To make mistakes, to learn, to grow.

Removing all of life's temptations would surely defeat that purpose, as well as slowing things down considerably.

Ho'oponopono practice has allowed me to understand that allowing a higher power, who loves me completely, who is part of myself, with infinite knowledge and wisdom, to make the right decisions for me, was the smartest thing I could ever do. Once my ego accepted that fact my life became so much easier.

I found peace...

Of course this is an ongoing struggle. My Conscious mind, my intellect, and ego still continue to believe in the illusion that it is they who are in control-

"Starve your ego, feed your soul"

It is important to remember that the Ho'oponopono process works because it corresponds to the *natural laws of the Universe*. It's *not magic* and it doesn't work some of the time- it works every time if we have used our knowledge and skills correctly.

Does an electrician question the fallibility of electricity?

If a bulb doesn't come after he's replaced it he realises that it is a fault with his work. He doesn't doubt the existence and power of electricity!

When you apply the Ho'oponopono process you are working with exact laws that enable you to harness the power of the Universe just as the electrician does and to achieve the correct results you must have the same level of faith and belief in the success of the process as that electrician has in the truth of electricity.

Chapter 8

Who's Who In Ho'oponopono?

The following people have all played major roles in the development, promotion and understanding of Ho'oponopono throughout the world, while they all have slightly different approaches to the practice. They all have at their core, the same wonderful message of forgiveness, redemption and hope, and they have all in their own way taught me to see the world with different eyes.

My love and gratitude to them all.

Morrnah Simeona: born in Hawaii in 1913, is largely responsible for updating and establishing the foundations of modern Ho'oponopono.

Her mother was a *Kahuna* to Queen Lili'ukalani the last monarch of Hawaii.

Kahunas, roughly translated as Ka *(light)* and Huna *(secret)*, or *keepers of the secret* were important and highly respected members of Hawaiian communities, performing the role of priest or shaman. They became the depositories of all the accumulated oral wisdom, and knowledge passed down from their ancestors. Their main function was to heal and solve community problems, and to do this they employed an ancient practice of reconciliation and forgiveness.

Morrnah grew up immersed in these ancient traditions, and spiritual practices. She began her Kahuna instruction at age three, and began a lifetime of learning and teaching. In 1976 when she was 63 years old, and reacting to modern day changes, Morrnah began to adapt the process to more suit the demands of the modern world.

One of the *fundamental changes* being that it could now *be practised individually.*

This is how she described the new updated process as follows-

"Ho'oponopono is a profound gift which allows one to develop a working relationship with the Divinity within and learn to ask that in each moment, our errors in thought, word, deed or action be cleansed. The process is essentially about freedom, complete freedom from the past." - Morrnah Nalamaku Simeona, Kahuna Lapa'au [59]

She called the process Self Identity through Ho'oponopono (SITH), and in 1980 she announced the new healing process to the world at the World Huna Conference in Hawaii.

She spent the rest of her life teaching, writing, and promoting Ho'oponopono around the world, setting up the *Foundation of 'I'* - a major centre for Ho'oponopono studies and teaching based in Hawaii. She has given speeches on Ho'oponopono to both the United Nations, and the World Health Organisation.

In 1983 Morrnah was officially recognised as a *Kahuna Lapa'au* and honoured as *"National Living Treasure of Hawaii"*. She passed over in 1992, at the age of 79.

Dr Hew Len: As mentioned earlier Dr Ihaleakala Hew Len Ph.D. studied under Morrnah at the Foundation of I for many years and currently is the foundations' Chairman Emeritus. He holds a Ph.D from the University of Iowa, a B.Sc from the University of Idaho, and a B.A from the University of Colorado.

One of the main principles of his teachings is that we only have to remember one thing when encountering problems in life; that **"Peace begins with me"**.

In order to bring peace to the world, we first have to bring peace to ourselves. We are not only responsible for our own actions, and circumstances, but for everyone else's as well. Everything we see and experience is a reflection of ourselves, only by changing ourselves can we change the world around us. Only by healing ourselves first, can we heal others.

Dr Len continued where Morrnah left off, further developing and updating the modern version of Ho'oponopono which he now called Self-I-Dentity Through Ho'oponopono (SITH), placing much more emphasis on the personal responsibility aspect of the process.

Dr Len teaches that the ultimate aim of the Ho'oponopno practioner is to erase (clean) his/her subconcious minds in order to reach a *"State of Zero"*. In this state which he calls *Zero Limits* we are limitless, memory free, and open to inspirational thoughts flowing down from Divine Intelligence through our super-conscious minds.

Ho'oponopono practice not only cleans and clears our minds and improves our receptivity, it also gives us a direct connection to greatest source of power, wisdom and knowledge imaginable- Universal Consciousness. It is this power that all of mankind's greatest human endeavours have originated from.

"Zero Limits" is also the title of his bestselling book, collaboration with metaphysical author and speaker Joe Vitale, which received rave reviews when it was published in 1997.

The book and its sequel *"At Zero"* were both worldwide successes, striking a cord with millions around the world. The book collaboration between Dr Hew Len and Joe has probably done more to promote the spread of Ho'oponopono than any other publication.

Below is Joe Vitale's fascinating account of how he first discovered Dr Hew Len and the modern Ho'oponopono process, courtesy of Dr Joe Vitale @ http://www.mrfire.com -

"Two years ago, I heard about a therapist in Hawaii who cured a complete ward of criminally insane patients--without ever seeing any of them. The psychologist would study an inmate's chart and then look within himself to see how he created that person's illness. As he improved himself, the patient improved.

When I first heard this story, I thought it was an urban legend. How could anyone heal anyone else by healing himself? How could even the best self-improvement master cure the criminally insane?

It didn't make any sense. It wasn't logical, so I dismissed the story.

However, I heard it again a year later. I heard that the therapist had used a Hawaiian healing process called ho'oponopono. I had never heard of it, yet I couldn't let it leave my mind. If the story was at all true, I had to know more.

I had always understood "total responsibility" to mean that I am responsible for what I think and do. Beyond that, it's out of my hands. I think that most people think of total responsibility that way. We're responsible for what we do, not what anyone else does. The Hawaiian therapist who healed those mentally ill people would teach me an advanced new perspective about total responsibility.

His name is Dr. Ihaleakala Hew Len. We probably spent an hour talking on our first phone call. I asked him to tell me the complete story of his work as a therapist. He explained that he worked at Hawaii State Hospital for four years. That ward where they kept the criminally insane was dangerous. Psychologists quit on a monthly basis. The staff called in sick a lot or simply quit. People would walk through that ward with their backs against the wall, afraid of being attacked by patients. It was not a pleasant place to live, work, or visit.

Dr. Len told me that he never saw patients. He agreed to have an office and to review their files. While he looked at those files, he would work on himself. As he worked on himself, patients began to heal.

"After a few months, patients that had to be shackled were being allowed to walk freely," he told me. "Others who had to be heavily medicated were getting off their medications. And those who had no chance of ever being released were being freed."

I was in awe.

"Not only that," he went on, "but the staff began to enjoy coming to work. Absenteeism and turnover disappeared. We ended up with more staff than we needed because patients were being released, and all the staff was showing up to work. Today, that ward is closed."

This is where I had to ask the million dollar question: "What were you doing within yourself that caused those people to change?"

"I was simply healing the part of me that created them," he said.

I didn't understand.

Dr. Len explained that total responsibility for your life means that everything in your life - simply because it is in your life--is your responsibility. In a literal sense the entire world is your creation.

Whew. This is tough to swallow. Being responsible for what I say or do is one thing. Being responsible for what everyone in my life says or does is quite another. Yet, the truth is this: if you take complete responsibility for your life, then everything you see, hear, taste, touch, or in any way experience is your responsibility because it is in your life.

This means that terrorist activity, the president, the economy--anything you experience and don't like--is up for you to heal. They don't exist, in a manner of speaking, except as projections from inside you. The problem isn't with them, it's with you, and to change them, you have to change you.

I know this is tough to grasp, let alone accept or actually live. Blame is far easier than total responsibility, but as I spoke with Dr. Len, I began to realize that healing for him and in

ho 'oponopono means loving yourself. If you want to improve your life, you have to heal your life. If you want to cure anyone--even a mentally ill criminal--you do it by healing you.

I asked Dr. Len how he went about healing himself. What was he doing, exactly, when he looked at those patients' files?

"I just kept saying, 'I'm sorry' and 'I love you' over and over again," he explained.

That's it?

That's it.

Turns out that loving yourself is the greatest way to improve yourself, and as you improve yourself, your improve your world.

Let me give you a quick example of how this works: one day, someone sent me an email that upset me. In the past I would have handled it by working on my emotional hot buttons or by trying to reason with the person who sent the nasty message. This time, I decided to try Dr. Len's method. I kept silently saying, "I'm sorry" and "I love you," I didn't say it to anyone in particular. I was simply evoking the spirit of love to heal within me what was creating the outer circumstance.

Within an hour I got an e-mail from the same person. He apologized for his previous message. Keep in mind that I didn't take any outward action to get that apology. I didn't even write him back. Yet, by saying "I love you," I somehow healed within me what was creating him... If you want to improve anything in your life, there's only one place to look; inside you.. "

And *"When you look, do it with love"* Dr Hew Len (53)

Copyright © 2005 by Joe Vitale (54)

Dr Joe Vitale: As mentioned above Dr Len teamed up with Dr Joe Vitale to publish *"Zero Limits"* . Joe is probably best known for his work on the million selling book sensation "The Secret" and the subsequent movie of the same name. Joe is a prolific author and extremely successful marketer. His skills have helped considerably in spreading the Ho'oponopono process around the world.

After first hearing of Dr Hew Len's Ho'oponopono work on a group of mentally disabled inmates in the Hawaiian prison system. He tracked him down and began to study under him, culminating in their book collaborations. I particularly like his reaction when first learning the technique-

"There are moments in Ho'oponopono that make you question reality"- Joe Vitale [55]

Mabel Katz: Mabel is another author and lecturer who has done much to spread the teachings of modern Ho'oponopono. She studied the Self-I-Dentity process under Dr Len at The Foundation of I for twelve years in the 1990s eventually becoming a teacher herself.

In 2004 she gained permission to use the process in her own teachings and branched out on her own. Since then she has written many successful books, including her best-selling series on Ho'oponopono *"The Easiest Way"*.

Mabel is Argentine and many of her books have been published in Spanish as well. Currently based in Los Angeles she travels all over the world holding workshops and seminars on Ho'oponopono.

'Aunty' Malia Craver: b. 1927-2009. Another Hawaiian native and Ho'oponopono teacher, who was venerated by the Hawaiian people as a *"National Living Treasure"* during her lifetime.

She spent over 30 years working in children's centres and used Ho'oponopono daily in her work with vulnerable children. In 2000 she gave a speech on Ho'oponopono to the United Nations.

Robert F. Ray: Author of *"Return to Zeropoint,"* Robert has been a student of the noetic sciences, psychology, religion and Eastern philosophy for more than 25 years. An ordained Old Catholic priest, and Franciscan contemplative, his focus has been on alleviating suffering in those who are poor, sick, marginalised and emotionally wounded. He is an accomplished Ho'oponopono practitioner and gives regular seminars and classes on the subject from his home in Florida USA.

Sondra Ray: Renowned spiritual teacher Sondra is probably best known for her work on conscious breathing and during the 1970s she was a pioneer in the widely acclaimed rebirthing technique. Today as well as writing she and her husband Markus give lectures and workshops on the metaphysical classic *"A Course in Miracles"*.

What is not as well know is that Sondra studied Ho'oponopono under Morrnah Simeona herself which resulted in her book "Pele's Wish" in which she gives an excellent account of her experiences with the *Kahuna's* on Hawaii.

Chapter 9

Other Ho'oponopono Tools

While it is true that we need nothing but our minds and the four phrases to practice Ho'oponopono- Dr Hew Len advises that practice can be complimented and/or enhanced by adopting the following habits:

Breathing exercise; 2 times a day breath in for 7 seconds, hold for 7 seconds, breath out for 7 seconds, hold for 7 seconds. That is 1 cycle. Repeat 9 times.

Blue solar water; keep your body as hydrated as possible, preferably with water that has been stored in a blue glass bottle and infused with natural sunlight.

Strawberries and Blueberries; these fruits are recommended by Dr Len as particularly good in facilitating the Ho'oponopono process.

Ho'oponopono and Meditation; meditation is perfect for creating the calm, open, receptive conditions that Ho'oponopono needs to flourish. Use your daily meditative techniques in combination with your petitions to compliment the process. Combine with the breathing exercises for even better results.

"If your mind is empty, it is always ready for anything; it is open to everything. In the beginner's mind there are many possibilities, in the expert's mind there are few." - Shunryu Suzuki, (1904-1971) [56]

Ceeport; a selection of items such as labels, pins, stickers, cards designed to assist in cleaning objects and people. Ceeport stands for Clean, Erase, Erase, Return to Port (Zero).

To date I have not had any first- hand experience of the effectiveness of Ceeport, If you do decide to give it a try then I would love to hear your thoughts @ http://ho-oponopono-explained.com. They are available to purchase through Dr Hew Len's website- http://ihhl-ceeport.com

Chapter 10

Final Thoughts

One of the things that grabbed me when I first discovered Ho'oponopono was the wonderful simplicity of it. It made sense. Only a Divine Intelligence could design something so elegant and simple, the perfect solution for its purpose.

Ho'oponopono's core belief that each and every one of us is a powerful, eternal, spiritual being. That we are entirely responsible for all that we are, all we experience, struck a chord with me. I didn't need to look outside myself. I didn't have to follow a guru or master.

The answer was inside me all along-

"Who looks outside, dreams. Who looks inside, awakes." - Carl Jung [57]

While it's true that we can't stop karmatic events from affecting us in this life. They still have to be resolved, and their lessons learned.

We can however choose how we deal with them...

The Universe is a benign, and loving place. It would not create a life where our only choice is to sit helpless, waiting for the storms of life to hit us. The Universe is not vengeful. It doesn't want to hurt us. It's on our side. It wants us to learn our lessons.

It wants us to succeed!

It's up to us whether we do it the easy way or the hard way. It loves us so much that it won't ever violate **our free will!** It's our choice alone...

If we are deliberately making a *conscious effort* to resolve our karma, if we are *trying* to evolve, and going in the right direction, then fate will leave us alone to go our own way, at our own pace...

If the lesson has been learned, we don't have to repeat it.

If you do find yourself repeating the same mistakes over and over, then pay close attention for there is something that you have not learned from that situation, and until you do you will be unable to move on.

If we face up to our past mistakes and take action to resolve them, then we are free to move on to the next challenge...

It is only when we get *stuck in a rut*, making little or no progress that The Universe will give us the kick up the backside we need to get us going! And it will continue to do so, with even more dramatic events, until we **pay attention...!**

The Ho'oponopono process gives us the tools we need to resolve these karmatic problems in a gentler, less dramatic way. It puts the power back in your hands, it gives you control, and brings you peace while the storm rages around you...

The growing trend towards individualistic methods of worship has put the power back in the hands of the people. No longer are we blindly following others. The world is waking up, slowly realising the illusion that surrounds us, and the knowledge of our true selves.

I believe that the Ho'oponopono process has come to us at exactly the right time to assist us in our own, and mankind's, spiritual evolution and ascension. Practising Ho'oponopono regularly will open up many new possibilities and opportunities in your life if you give it your full focus and attention- the rest is up to you.

I hope that this book answered some of your initial questions about the process, enough at least to get you started on your own Ho'oponopono adventure. I wish you well on your journey, and leave you with one final thought to remember when things get tough-

"You are a powerful, eternal, spiritual Being of light...

Here on Earth to experience all there is...

Nothing you can do is wrong...

You are loved completely...

Chapter 11

Inspiration, Thanks, & Acknowledgements

Firstly thanks for purchasing this book and reading it through to the end. I'd love to hear any comments or feedback you might have.

You can contact me on the social media sites:

Facebook - https://www.facebook.com/HooponoponoSecrets

Twitter - https://twitter.com/Hoponosecrets

E-Mail - ianpauljackson1111@gmail.com

For more information, articles and discussion on Ho'oponopono you very welcome to visit my blog - www.ho-oponopono-explained.com

One small favour please; if you have enjoyed this book and would like to help me spread the Ho'oponopono message to as many people as possible, you can do so by writing me a quick review here on Amazon - http://www.amazon.com/gp/product/B00OGOBR2G

I Love You..Thank You..

Paul Jackson

Inspiration & Sources

Below you will find a list of the sources and teachers whose hard work and dedication to spreading, and teaching, spiritual awareness around the world have been my inspiration. I highly recommend reading their works and following their teachings

This book is a result of my own experiences in practising Ho'oponopono, and my personal interpretation of theirs, and others' teachings. My love and thanks to them all.

Morrnah Simeona - http://www.amazingwomeninhistory.com/mor-rnah-nalamaku-simeona-hawaiian-healer

Dr Ihaleakala Hew Len - http://www.self-i-dentity-through-hoopono-pono.com

Dr Joe Vitale - http://www.zerolimits.info

Aloha Gary - https://alohagary.wordpress.com

Serge Kahili King - http://www.sergeking.com

Darryl Anka (Bashar) - http://bashar.org

Dr Brian Weiss - http://www.brianweiss.com

Michael Newton Ph.D. - http://newtoninstitute.org

Eckhart Tolle - https://www.eckharttolle.com

Tania Kotsos - http://www.mind-your-reality.com

Wayne Dyer - http://www.drwaynedyer.com

Rhonda Bryne - http://thesecret.tv

Lobsang Rampa - http://www.lobsangrampa.org

Prof Tor Norretranders - http://www.tor.dk

Bruce Lipton Ph.D. - https://www.brucelipton.com

Buddha - http://en.wikipedia.org/wiki/Gautama_Buddha

Carl Jung - http://www.carl-jung.net

Jesus - http://en.wikipedia.org/wiki/Jesus

Edgar Cayce - http://www.edgarcayce.org

Uell S. Anderson - http://www.mentorsofnewthought.com/mentors/uell-stanley-andersen

Tania Kotsos - http://www.mind-your-reality.com

The Dalai Lama - http://www.dalailama.com

Abraham Hicks - http://www.abraham-hicks.com

Alan Watts - http://alanwatts.com/

Eben Alexander - http://www.ebenalexander.com

Joseph Murphy - http://en.wikipedia.org/wiki/Joseph_Murphy

Claude M. Bristol - http://claudebristol.wwwhubs.com

Robert Collier - http://robertcollier.wwwhubs.com

James Allen - http://jamesallen.wwwhubs.com/think.htm

Earl Nightingale - http://www.earlnightingale.com

Charles F. Haanel - http://www.haanel.com

William Shakespeare - http://www.william-shakespeare.info

Nikolas Tesla - http://en.wikipedia.org/wiki/Nikola_Tesla

Ernest Holmes - http://en.wikipedia.org/wiki/Ernest_Holmes

Hermes Trismegistus - http://en.wikipedia.org/wiki/Hermeticism

Plato - http://en.wikipedia.org/wiki/Plato

Erika L. Soul - http://dailydivineblessings.blogspot.co.uk

Greg Calise - http://riverbankoftruth.com

Special Love & Thanks to my editors for their hard work and insight:

Caroline Donahue, Anne Marie Nichol, & Katerina El Haj.

ACKNOWLEDGEMENTS:

[1] - Miracles and Inspiration.com

[2]- [34] [57]- C.G. Jung

[3]- [8] - Ernest Holmes

[4]- [10] [22] [48] [52]- Albert Einstein

[5] - Erwin Schrodinger

[6] - Plato

[7]- [47] [50]- Nikola Tesla

[9] - Michelangelo.com

[11]- Hermes Trismegistus

[12]- The Kybalion

[13]- Ecclesiastes

[14]- Heraclitus Wiki

[15]- Greg Calise

[16]- Dalai Lama

[17]- Jesus

[18]- [36] [39]- Buddha

[19]- The Bible

[20]- Eugene Delacroix

[21]- Sir Isaac Newton

[23]- <u>Ralph Waldo Emerson</u>

[24]- <u>Pablo Picasso</u>

[25]- [32] [46]- <u>Bashar</u>

[26]- <u>Mahatma Gandhi</u>

[27]- [31] [40] [41] [42] [43] [45]- <u>Tor Nørretranders</u>

[28]- <u>Jack London</u>

[29]- <u>Isaac Bashevis Singer</u>

[30]- <u>epictetus</u>

[33]- <u>Paul Levy</u>

[35]- <u>Phil Cousineau</u>

[37]- <u>Herman Melville</u>

[38]- [53]- <u>Zero Limits</u>

[44]- <u>Alan Watts</u>

[49]- <u>John Hagelin</u>

[51]- [56]- <u>SITH</u>

[54]- [55]- <u>Joe Vitale</u>

[56]- <u>Shunryu Suzuki</u>

[58]- <u>C.S. Lewis</u>

[59]- [60]- <u>The Foundation of I</u>

[61]- <u>U. S Andersen</u>

About the Author

Paul has spent most of his life with a serious case of wanderlust. He has travelled, lived, or worked in over 30 countries around the world.

He served in the British Forces for 7 years, and after discharge gained an Honours Degree in South East Asian Studies. Paul studied Thai language for a year at Chiang Mai University and then went on to teach English and Tourism. He currently lives in the UK and is father to an 11 year old princess…

For all the latest Ho'oponopono news, articles, and discussion visit Paul's blog – www.Ho-oponopono-Explained.com

Join Me On Facebook- HooponoponoSecrets

Follow Me On Twitter @Hoponosecrets

E-Mail- ianpauljackson1111@gmail.com

Ho'oponopono Links

Self I-Dentity Through Ho'oponopono - http://www.self-i-dentity-through-hooponopono.com

The Foundation of I - http://www.hooponopono.org

Sondra Ray - https://www.sondraray.com

Robert F. Ray - http://www.returntozeropoint.com

Ulrich E. Dupree - https://www.goodreads.com/author/show/5813408. Ulrich_E_Dupree

Mabel Katz - http://www.mabelkatz.com

Dr Joe Vitale - http://www.zerolimits.info

Dr Hew Len - http://zero-wise.com

Aloha Gary - https://alohagary.wordpress.com

Max Freedom Long - http://www.maxfreedomlong.com

Kelly Martin - http://www.kellymartinspeaks.co.uk

Barb Hindley - http://hooponoponolife.blogspot.co.uk

Serge Kahili King - http://www.sergeking.com

Huna - http://www.huna.org

Erika L. Soul - http://dailydivineblessings.blogspot.co.uk

Mantras & Prayers

One of the first problems I had when I started practising Ho'oponopono was formulating the petitions. There are very few examples of practical mantras that outline how exactly to word the petitions especially for specific issues.

The examples that are available are commonly very religious in their wording. In this section I have a listed a selection of Ho'oponopono prayers and petitions that will hopefully give you some ideas and inspiration.

First, two of Morrnah Simeona's original prayers courtesy of *The Foundation of I-* [60]

The Peace Of «I»

Ka Maluhia o ka «I»

Peace be with you, All My Peace,

O ka Maluhia no me oe, Ku›u Maluhia a pau loa,

The Peace that is « I «, the Peace that is «I am».

Ka Maluhia o ka «I», owau no ka Maluhia,

The Peace for always, now and forever and evermore.

Ka Maluhia no na wa a pau, no ke›ia wa a mau a mau loa aku.

My Peace « I « give to you, My Peace « I « leave with you,

Ha›awi aku wau I ku›u Maluhia ia oe, waiho aku wau I ku›u Maluhia me oe,

Not the world›s Peace, but, only My Peace,

The Peace of « I «.

A›ole ka Maluhia o ke ao aka, ka›u Maluhia wale no,

Ka Maluhia o ka «I»

———————

"I" Am The "I"

Owau no ka "I"

"I" come forth from the void into light,

Pua mai au mai ka po iloko o ka malamalama,

"I" am the breath that nurtures life,

Owau no ka ha, ka mauli ola,

"I" am that emptiness, that hollowness beyond all consciousness,

Owau no ka poho, ke ka'ele mawaho a'e o no ike apau.

The "I", the Id, the All.

Ka I, Ke Kino Iho, na Mea Apau.

"I" draw my bow of rainbows across the waters,

Ka a'e au i ku'u pi'o o na anuenue mawaho a'e o na kai a pau,

The continuum of minds with matters.

Ka ho'omaumau o na mana'o ame na mea a pau.

"I" am the incoming and outgoing of breath,

Owau no ka "Ho", a me ka "Ha"

The invisible, untouchable breeze,

He huna ka makani nahenahe,

The undefinable atom of creation.

Ka "Hua" huna o Kumulipo.

"I" am the "I".

Owau no ka "I".

HO'OPONOPONO MANTRAS

The following mantras are ones that I used at some point in my practice. They should give you an idea of the structure and content to use in your Ho'oponopono practice. As you practice you will develop your own unique style and wording relevant to your own life.

If you would like to share your mantras with the Ho'oponopono community your welcome to post them on my Mantra Page @ Ho'oponopono-Explained.com

General:

Morning Mantra-

I Love You...

I'm Sorry for anything I have ever done in this life or any other, consciously or unconsciously, to hurt or harm or cause pain to anyone or anything...

Please Forgive me...

Thank You...

Evening Mantra-

I Love You...

Thank You for my existence, this wonderful opportunity to live in these times. Thank You for the love that surrounds me, my family and friends. Thank You for all the people you sent to help me on my way. Thank You for my health and strength, my passion for life. Thank You for the opportunities in my life, the excitement and adventure. Thank You for the peace and kindness in my life and for my wisdom and patience. Thank You for all that I am, all that I have, and all I'm about to receive...

Help me spend my time here wisely...

Thank You...

————————

Abundance:

I Love You Success, I Love having you in my life..

I Love the validation you bring, the platform you give me to build my dreams. I Love excitement and joy you bring, and the adventures you take me on...

I'm Sorry for anything I have ever done to block you from my life, either consciously or unconsciously, in this life or any other. I'm Sorry if I've neglected you or taken you for granted. I'm Sorry if I have judged you in any way...

Please Forgive me...

Thank You...

————————

I Love You Money, I Love having you in my life. I Love the comfort and hope you bring, the security, happiness, and opportunities you create, the platform you give me to build my dreams on. I Love the excitement, the happiness, and adventure you bring. I Love the friends you help me find and the Love you help me spread.

I'm Sorry for anything I have ever done, consciously or unconsciously, to cause you hurt or harm, in this life or any other. I'm Sorry if I have abused or misused you, I'm Sorry if I have taken you for granted or not appreciated you. I'm Sorry if I have judged you. I'm Sorry for anything I ever done to blocked you from my life...

Please Forgive me...

Thank You...

Well-Being:

I Love You Health & Strength, I Love the confidence you give me, the tasks you help me accomplish...

I'm Sorry for anything I have ever done to cause a lack of you in my life. I'm Sorry if I haven't appreciated your wonderful gifts...

Please Forgive me...

Thank You...

Relationships:

I Love You Passion & Romance. I Love the excitement and adventure you bring to my life, I Love the warmth and comfort, the friend-ship and the Love...

I'm Sorry for anything I have ever done to cause a lack of you in my life. I'm sorry if i have blocked your wonderful gifts from my life in any way, consciously or unconsciously, In this life or nay other...

Please Forgive me...

Thank You...

I Love You Confidence and Charisma. I Love the adventures you take me on, the doors you open, and the possibilities you create. I Love the friends you help me meet and the lovers you help me find. I Love the Strength and courage you give me...

I'm Sorry for anything I have ever done to block you from my life, consciously or unconsciously, in the life or any other...

Please Forgive me...

Thank You...

Other People:

I Love You _____. I Love you for your friendship, your support, your unconditional love for me...

I'm Sorry for anything I have ever done to cause your hurt, harm, or pain, consciously or unconsciously, in this life or any of my previous lives....

Please Forgive me...

Thank You...

Thank You _____. Thank You for your love and support. Thank you for the wisdom and comfort you bring the my life, the fun and laughter. Thank you for loving me un-conditionally.

I'm Sorry for hurting you, for causing you pain...

Please Forgive me...

Thank You...

Inanimate Objects:

I Love You room...

Thank You for giving me comfort and shelter. Thank You for your warmth and generosity...

I'm Sorry if I have offended or harmed you in any way...

Please Forgive me...

Nature :

Thank You Mother Gaia. Thank you for the warm sunshine on my face...

I'm Sorry if I have taken you for granted and not appreciated your wonderful gifts...

Please Forgive me...

I Love You...

Gratitude:

I Love You_____.

Thank You...

Repeat.. Repeat.. Repeat..

———————

And finally a wonderful meditation prayer from Uell. S Andersen, in his book "Three Magic Words" -

"I turn away from the world about me to the world of Consciousness that lies within. I shut out all memories of the past, create no images of the future. I concentrate on my being, on my awareness. I slide deep into the very recesses of my soul to a place of utter repose. Here I perceive faith in the making, am conscious of the one being from which all beings spring. I know that this immortal Self, this is God, this is me. I am, I always was, I always will be. All men, all things, all space and time and life are here in the depths of my soul. Smaller than small, greater than great meet and unite in me. That which I thought I was, ego, I never was at all, for it was a changing thing, mirroring the seasons and the tides, a thing to be born and grow and die. I am not a thing of time or circumstance. I am spirit, pure and eternal, birthless, deathless and changeless. I am patient, for I am all time. I am wise, for I contain the knowledge of all things. I know not pain, for I see there is no beginning and no end, and who suffers pain must see beginning and end. I am rich, for there is no limit to the abundance I may create from my very Self. I am successful, for I need only think to achieve. I love and am beloved, for all things are myself and I am all things. I unite, I fuse, I become one with Universal Subconscious Mind. The mask of vanity and ego I shall never wear again. I perceive the magnificent Dweller at the centre of my consciousness, and I know Him to

be my very self. Time and space, shadow and substance, what matter these? I am God."

Andersen, Uell S, (1917-1986). *"Three Magic Words"* [61]

CPSIA information can be obtained at www.ICGtesting.com
Printed in the USA
LVOW07s1057151015

458399LV00019B/249/P